CW00498273

Very Simple
CHINESE
An Introduction to Mandarin

Language and Etiquette

Kim Winfield

STACEY
INTERNATIONAL

Very Simple
CHINESE
An Introduction to Mandarin

Language and Etiquette

STACEY
INTERNATIONAL

VERY SIMPLE CHINESE

Stacey International
128 Kensington Church Street
London W8 4BH
Tel: + 44 (0) 20 7221 7166
Fax: + 44 (0) 20 7792 9288
E-mail: info@stacey-international.co.uk
Website: www.stacey-international.co.uk

© 2008 Kim Winfield & Paul Gillam

1 3 5 7 9 8 6 4 2

ISBN: 978-1-905299-47-8

Written by Kim Winfield
Illustrated by Paul Gillam

Printed in Dubai

All rights reserved. No part of this publication may be
reproduced or transmitted in any form or by any means
without the permission of the copyright owners.

British Library Catalogue in Publication Data:
A catalogue record for this book is available from
the British Library.

INTRODUCTION

Spoken Chinese is tonal. The national language, 'Potunghua' or 'Mandarin', has four tones and the Southern dialect, Cantonese, even more. On the written side, a form of romanisation, Pin Yin, is usually learned first as a stepping stone to learning Chinese characters. Therefore acquiring any degree of proficiency in this language especially requires time, aptitude and application.

For many visitors to China, the prospect of learning even a little of the language is too daunting. This, therefore, is not a 'teach yourself Chinese' book. It is a highly selective phrase book and guide to simple etiquette for the tourist or businessman visiting China with minimal time and effort to spare. It does not address tones and uses a simple and unique romanisation system.

In the context the phrases and vocabulary are used, pronounce the words clearly as they are spelled in the text and you will be understood. The book is designed to be helpful, entertaining and accessible to the casual student of Chinese. As in many other countries, but especially in China, the smallest efforts by a foreigner to learn the language, customs and etiquette are greatly appreciated.

Whatever the purpose of your visit to this fascinating country, a little time reading this book will be richly rewarded.

ACKNOWLEDGEMENTS

I am greatly indebted to Sir James Hodge KCMG, Max Scott and Kitty Carruthers for their kind advice and support, and, especially, to Paul Gillam for his excellent artistry and unfailing good humour.

KW

CONTENTS

A Note on the Transliteration

The national language of China, "Mandarin" or "Potunghua", and all the many dialects, are tonal. The tone is basically an inflection, rising, falling or level, in pronounciation. The same word has different meanings according to the tone in which it is pronounced. For example, "tar" can mean to trample, a pagoda or he, she, or it. "Tee" can mean to carry, to shave or to kick. Learning and pronouncing the tones accurately is a key factor for the serious student of Chinese.

However, the visiting tourist or businessman may not have the time or inclination to master the tones. Therefore the selected phrases in this book can be used without tones. In the context the phrases are used, simply pronounce the words slowly and clearly as they are spelled in English in the text. You will be understood.

Be prepared to repeat yourself to overcome an initial surprise that you are speaking Chinese!

1
On Arrival

General greeting

Knee how?
Hello, are you well?

Hen how, share share knee.
Very well, thank you.

Welcome

Wan ying knee.
Welcome.

Share share knee.
Thank you.

Good morning

Jow.
(colloquial greeting and reply)
Good morning. Hello.

Good evening

Wang shang how.
(on leaving)
Good evening.

How are you?

Knee how. Shen tea how ma?
How are you? In good health?

Han how, share share knee.
Very well, thank you.

And you?

Knee nay?
And you?

War doe hen how.
I am well too.

Goodbye

Zai gen. (on leaving)
Goodbye. (*lit.* see you again)

Man man jow.
Mind how you go.

See you tomorrow

Ming tian gen.
See you again tomorrow.

Some useful phrases:

Please
Cheng knee

Thank you
Share share knee

What is your name?
Knee gwai sing ma? (formal)
Knee jow sher mer ming zer? (colloquial)

My name is Joe Bloggs
See-how sing Joe Bloggs (formal)
War jow Joe Bloggs (colloquial)

Do you speak English?
Knee shore ying you ma?

I don't understand
War boo ming buy

That is mine
Zer share war der

Where is the taxi?
Dick sea zai nar?

Bus
Gung gong chee cher

Train
Wore cher

Rental car
Chew zoo chee cher

Toilet
Chee sore

I have one bag missing
Ye ger sing lee boo yow

How much is that?
Door see-how cheen?

Where is my luggage?
War der sing lee zai nar?

2
Getting Around

In a taxi

Cheng knee, dow 'Hay Ye Done' loo gwan chew.
To the Hilton Hotel, please.

Doi, see-how jer. May yow when tee.
Yes, Miss. No problem.

Door see-how cheen?
How much?

Er sher kwai.
Twenty Renmenbi.

Boo how. Tie gwooi.
No, that's too much.

How, sher woo kwai.
OK, fifteen Renmenbi then.

How hen door!
That's much better!

8

Dow loo gwan, door see-how gong lee?
How many kilometres to the hotel?

Sher san ger, seen shang.
Thirteen, Sir.

If you wish to give directions:

Cheng knee, ye gee chew.
Go straight ahead, please.

Cheng knee, jaw bien chew.
Please go to the left.

Cheng knee, you bien chew.
Please go to the right.

Cheng knee, jer lee teng cher.
Stop here, please.

Cheng knee, kwai ye dee ar.
Faster, please.

Cheng knee, maan ye dee ar.
Slower, please.

11

Cheng knee, jer lee deng ye deng.
Wait here, please.

War woo fen jong wooi lay.
I will be back in five minutes.

3
In the Hotel

Knee how?
Hello, how are you?

Hen how, share share knee.
Very well, thank you.

See-how sing Smith.
My name is Smith.

Wan ying knee lay, Smith Seen Shang.
Welcome, Mr Smith.

War yi jing ding jaw fang jian.
I have reserved a room.

Cheng knee, war yew fang jian.
I require a room, please.

*War yew schwang ren chuang fang jian,
gen yew fang.*
I require a double room with a bathroom
en suite.

Fan jian yow may yow kung chi tew jer ji?
Does the room have an air conditioner?

Yow. Door yow yin ter wang.
Yes. It also has internet access.

May tian der fang fey, door see-how cheen?
How much is the room per day?

Cheng knee, yow may yow pea-hen ye der fang jian?
Have you a cheaper room, please?

War yew dow fang jian, can ye can.
How boo how?
I wish to see the room. Is that OK?

Boo how. Doi boo chee.
War boo sea wan.
No. I'm sorry.
I don't like it at all.

17

Knee yow may yow jow how der fang jian?
Have you a better room?

Jer ger fang jian han how.
This room is fine.

Knee yew shen mer?
What do you want?

Ye ger seen sea, seen shang.
A message, Sir.

Cheng knee, deng ye deng.
Wait a moment, please.

Jean lay.
Come in.

Gay knee, seen shang.
For you, Sir.

What is my room number?
War der fang zer how sher shen mer?

My room number is ...
War der fang zer how sher ...

This is broken.
Jer share why ler.

My laundry.
War der see der dung see.

And when will it be ready?
Shen mer shee how see how ma?

I wish to leave this in the safe.
Jer ger, yew fang zai bow sian goy.

Where is the telephone?
Diane wah zai nar?

Have you any messages for me?
Knee yow seen sea gay war?

I require telephone number ...
War yew diane wah how ...

I want to post a letter.
War yew gee seen.

I need to send a fax.
War yew song chuan gen.

Have you got an English newspaper?
Knee yow ying yew der bow gee ma?

I wish to change money.
War yew wan cheen.

I wish to change traveller's cheques.
War yew wan loo sing gee pew.

I need a taxi.
War yew dick sea.

I am in a hurry.
War chong mang.

The bill, please.
Cheng knee, my daan.

What is this?
Jer share shen mer?

There is some mistake here.
Jer lee yow chore wu.

4
Meeting and Greeting

Gay knee men, rer ching der wan ying.
A warm welcome to you all.

Gwore jang, tie cur chee.
You are too kind.

Knee how?
How are you?

War han how. Knee nay?
I am very well. And you?

War dough han how. Cheng chore.
I am well. Please have a seat.

Share share knee.
Thank you.

Cheng knee, her car fey, her char ma?
Please, would you like coffee or tea?

Door jer, her cha.
Thank you. Tea, please.
(this 'thank you' is for a gift or a kindness)

Cheng knee, chur door, chur door.
Please, eat some more food.

Door jer, war chur bough.
Thank you, I am replete.

Smith Tie Tie, knee yow high zer ma?
Mrs Smith, do you have any children?

Yow leurng ger. Er zer sher san shoi.
New er jiu shoi.
Yes, I have two. A son aged 13 and a
daughter aged 9.

Wong Seen Shang, knee jer hun der ma?
Mr Wong, are you married?

Boo jer hun der.
No, I am not married.

5
Shopping

Door see-how cheen?
How much?

Sher ye kwai.
Eleven Renmenbi.

Waa! War gay woo kwai.
What! I'll give you five Renmenbi.

Baa kwai, how boo how?
Eight Renmenbi, how's that?

Wore jer, dan share hen gwooi.
Maybe, but that's expensive.

Boo kwai! Hen pea-hen ye.
It's not expensive, it's very cheap.

Jer ger chang diane, kai ma?
Is this shop open?

Sea-hen zai gwan men. Ming tian, kai der.
It is closed now. It is open tomorrow.

Seen Shang, knee yew shen mer?
Do you want something, Sir?

War boo yew, gee can ye can.
No, I am only looking around.

Seen Shang, hen pea-hen yi, hen how. Gee gay knee!
Sir, so cheap and very good. Just for you!

Bu yew, share share knee. War ye jing yow!
No thank you. I already have one!

Cheng knee, you chew zai nar?
Nar lee
Where is the Post Office please?
There.

To ask 'where is ... ?',
put '*zai nar ... ?*' after the noun.

ATM	*Chew kwan gee*
Antiques	*Goo dung*
Bank	*Yin hang*
Bank (branch)	*Fen hang*
Bookshop	*Shoe dian*
Chemist	*Yow fang*
Clothes	*Ye foo*
Dry cleaning	*Gan see*
Flowers	*Wah*
Hotel	*Loo gwan, fan diane*
Jewellery	*Joo Bow*
Market	*Sher chang*
Newspapers	*Bow gee*
Perfume	*Shang shoi*
Photographs	*Siang pea-hen*
Railway station	*Wore cher jan*
Restaurant	*chan gwan, fang wan, gwan zer*
Shoes	*Sea-air zer*
Sports	*Yuan dong*
Theatre	*Joo chang*
Toilet	*Che sore*
Tourist Information Office	*Loo yo geee lieu chew*
Zoo	*Dong wu yuan*

29

A shop is '*shang diane*'. Just add this to the end of the noun: e.g.

Flower shop   *Wah siang diane*

Cheng knee, war yew my 'chen shan'
I want to buy a 'shirt' please.

Lay ye lay! War der siang diane shen mer chen shan door yow.
Come in! My shop has all sorts of shirts.

The words below may be substituted for 'shirt' in the previous sentence:

Ballpoint pen	*Yuan joo bee*
Book	*Shoe*
Cigarettes	*Siang yan*
Comb, brush	*Shoe zer*
Dictionary	*Gee dean*
Envelopes	*Sin feng*
Film (for camera)	*Jow pea-hen*
Guide book	*Loo yo shoe*
Hat	*Mao zer*
Map	*Dee too*
Newspaper	*Bow gee*
Pen	*Bee*
Pencil	*Chan bee*
Razor	*Tee sue dow*
Razor blades	*Tee sue dow dow pea-hen*
Toilet paper	*Way sheng gee*
Toothbrush	*Ya shoe-er*
Toothpaste	*Ya gow*
Towel	*Mao gin*

6
Travelling & Sightseeing

Cheng knee, bang mang.
Please help me.

Dang ren. May yow when tee.
Certainly. No problem.

Dick sea jan, zai nar?
Where is the taxi stand?

Zai jaw bien. Xian der loo.
First road on the left.

Yuan ma?
Is it far?

Bu yuan, gee woo fen jong.
Not far, only five minutes.

Dow nar lee, neng joo ma?
Can I walk there?

Doi. Gee san buy me.
Yes, it's only 300 metres.

Jer dick sea, yow bee-how ma?
Does this taxi have a meter?

Yow, sheen shang. Zai nar chew?
Yes, Sir. Where do you want to go?

Cheng knee, dow Goo Gung chew.
To the Forbidden City, please.

Cheng chore cher.
Please get in.

Roo cow zai nar?
Where's the entrance?

Nar lee. Pee-ow jar share chee kwai.
There. The ticket costs seven Renmenbi.

Cheng knee, dow .... chew.
Please go to ....

Any of the following places:

Tiananmen Square
Tian An Men gwang churng

Forbidden City (Imperial Place)
Goo Gung

Temple of Heaven
Tian Tan

Summer Palace
Yer Her Yuan

Bei Hai Park
Bay High Gung Yuan

China Travel Service
Jong Gwore Loo Sing Share

Friendship Store
Yow Ye Shang Diane

Great Hall of the People
Ren Men Dar Wui Tang

Great Wall
(Wan Lee) Chang Cheng

Chairman Mao's Mausoleum
Mao Zoo See Jee Nian Tang

Museum
Bow Woo Gwan

Old Summer Palace
Yuan Ming Yuan

Airport
Fey Chee Chang

Railway station
Wore Cher Jan

Bus station
Gung Gong Chee Cher Jan

7
At the Restaurant

Zai foo gin, yow chan gwan ma?
Is there a restaurant nearby?

Doi. Nar loo yow hen door.
Yes, there are many down that street.

Cheng knee, yow yong ying yew der chai dan ma?
Have you a menu in English, please?

Cheng, war yew dow char? Bu wooi yong kwai zer.
Could I have a knife and fork, please? I cannot use chopsticks.

War yew deng chai. War yew ...
I want to order now. I would like ...

Any (or all!) of the following:

Fruit juice	*Gwore zer*
Coca cola	*Core la*
Beer	*Pea chew*
Wine	*Poo tow chew*
Bottled water	*Ping juang shoi*
Coffee	*Car fey*
Tea	*Char*
Chopsticks	*Kwai zer*
Cup	*Bay zer*
Dumplings	*Jow zer*
Chicken	*Gee roo*
Eggs	*Gee dan*
Fish	*You*
Fruit	*Shui gwore*
Oranges	*Cheng*
Apples	*Ping gwore*
Boiled rice	*Buy fan*
Fried rice	*Chow fan*

Beef	*New roo*
Pork	*Chew roo*
Vegetables	*Shoe chai*
Ice	*Bing*
Glass tumbler	*Bow lee bay*
Green tea	*Loo char*
Jasmine tea	*More lee wah char*
Menu	*Chai dan*
Milk	*New nigh*
Sandwich	*San meng jee*
Knife	*Dow zer*
Fork	*Char zer*
Knife and fork	*Dow char*
Spoon	*Showe zer*
Duck	*Ya zer*
Hot (spicey)	*Laa*
Breakfast	*Jow chan*
Lunch	*Woo fan*
Dinner	*Wan fan*
Restaurant	*Fan gwan, chan gwan*
	(Colloquial *gwan zer*)
Dining room	*Fan ting*
To eat	*Cher (fan)*
Cheers!	*Gan bay!*
Bill, account	*My dan*

8
Some Useful Expressions

Aye yar!
Oh dear!

Doi boo chee!
Sorry!

War boo ming buy.
I don't understand.

Dang ran.
Of course.

May gwan she.
Don't mention it/Never mind.

Lao jar.
Excuse me (interrupting).

Ching when.
Excuse me (to get past).

Knee hen lee mao
You are very kind/polite.

Knee wooi shore Ying Yew (Han Yew) ma?
Do you speak English (Chinese)?

Yi di ar.
Only a little.

Fey chang gee how.
Excellent!

Gan bay!
Cheers!

Enquiries

War yew (dai foo).
I need a (doctor).

The following can be substituted in this sentence:

Dentist	*Ya Ye*
Police	*Jing Fang*
The Manager	*Jing Lee*
Ambulance	*Joo Hoo Cher*

Jer lee war yow teng tong.
I have a pain here.

War yow ...
I have ...

Stomach ache	*Do zer teng*
Headache	*Too tong*
Toothache	*Yar teng*

Yung Han Yew, jer sher shen mer?
What is this called in Chinese?

Cheng knee, jai shore.
Tell me again, please.

Jer yow shen mer ye ser?
What does this mean?

9
Numbers, Months & Days of the Week

Numbers

0	*ling*
1	*ye*
2	*er* (or as 'a pair': *leurng*)
3	*san*
4	*ser*
5	*woo*
6	*lieu*
7	*chee*
8	*bar*
9	*jiu*
10	*sher*
11	*sher ye* (literally 10 + 1)
12	*sher er*
13	*sher san*
14	*sher ser*
15	*sher woo*
16	*sher lieu*
17	*sher chee*
18	*sher bar*
19	*sher jiu*
20	*er sher* (literally 2 x 10)
30	*san sher*
40	*ser sher*
50	*woo sher*
60	*lieu sher*
70	*chee sher*
80	*bar sher*
90	*jiu sher*

100	*buy*
1000	*che-an*
10,000	*wan*
1 million	*buy wan*
	(literally 100 x 10,000)

Numbers are easily composed, e.g.

65	*lieu sher woo*
	(6 x 10 + 5)
29	*er sher jiu*
	(2 x 10 + 9)
347	*san buy ser sher chee*
	(3 x 100, 4 x 10, +7)
803	*bar buy san*
	(8 x 100 +3)
1422	*ye che-an ser buy er sher er*
	(1 x 1000, 4 x 100, 2 x 10, +2)

46

Days of the week

Monday	*Sing chee ye*
Tuesday	*Sing chee er*
Wednesday	*Sing chee san*
Thursday	*Sing chee ser*
Friday	*Sing chee woo*
Saturday	*Sing chee lieu*
Sunday	*Sing chee chee*

Day	*Tian*
Week	*Sing chee*
Month	*Yewer*
Year	*Nee-en*
Tomorrow	*Meng tian*
Yesterday	*Jaw tian*

Months

January	*Ye yewer*
February	*Er yewer*
March	*San yewer*
April	*Ser yewer*
May	*Woo yewer*
June	*Lieu yewer*
July	*Chee yewer*
August	*Bar yewer*
September	*Jiu yewer*
October	*Sher yewer*
November	*Sher ye yewer*
December	*Sher er yewer*

Telling the time

To tell the time, simply place the numbers before the hour (*diane*) and minutes (*fun*).

jiu diane

sher diane sher woo fun

bar diane san sher fun

san diane woo fun

10
The Chinese Zodiac

The Chinese Zodiac is based on a twelve year cycle, each year named after an animal. There are several explanations of the origin of the zodiac. One states that the Jade Emperor held a swimming race and that the first twelve animals across the river would each have a year named after them. The cunning rat asked the kindly ox to carry him across on his back. The ox agreed, but when he neared the far bank the rat leapt ashore ahead of him.

Hence the first year of the zodiac is named after the rat, with the poor ox tricked into second. Some people believe that you will have certain characteristics of the animal associated with the year of your birth, so do not be surprised if you are asked for these details.

Rat
Born in 1948, 1960, 1972, 1984, 1996, 2008

Ambitious, imaginative and charming. Very generous, loyal and caring to their family and close friends. Shrewd in business and careful with money. Enjoys lively company and can be boisterous. Sometimes can be over-critical and quick tempered, but does not bear malice. Future planning and long-term strategy is not a strong point.

Ox
Born in 1949, 1961, 1973, 1984, 1997

Born leaders endowed with great confidence, charisma and ambition. Dependable, conservative and somewhat predictable. Slow to anger, even-tempered and patient. Very loyal and demanding in their relationships, which tend to be long term, both professionally and socially. Tend to have a wide circle of acquaintances and a few good friends.

Tiger
Born in 1950, 1962, 1974, 1986, 1998

Flamboyant, sensitive, emotional and romantic. Very confident, versatile and positive. Seldom downcast or weary, thriving on new challenges, risky ventures and the unknown. Good leaders rather than followers, with an inherent dislike for taking orders or conformity. Very generous, forgiving and outgoing, but can be impetuous, stubborn and rebellious.

Rabbit
Born in 1951, 1963, 1975, 1987, 1999

Always affectionate, caring and sensitive. Enjoys strong family ties and friendships. Very astute with a good business acumen and hidden resilience under pressure. Peace makers who avoid confrontation if possible. Cautious, conservative and refined, enjoying life's pleasures to the full. However, can sometimes be sentimental and emotionally vulnerable.

Dragon
Born in 1952, 1964, 1976, 1988, 2000

Ambitious, hard working and determined to succeed. Intelligent, gifted and fun loving. Enjoys life to the full. Always popular with all, dynamic and positive. Considered to be the luckiest of all the zodiac animals. However, can be capricious and foolhardy, resisting advice and resenting criticism.

Snake
Born in 1953, 1965, 1977, 1989, 2001

Blessed with abundant charm, wisdom and wit. A perfectionist for whom only the best is good enough. Patient, good humoured and a deep thinker. Good at making money and even better at keeping it. Shrewd and rather parsimonious. Slow to make friends and wary of lasting relationships. However, thrives on good company and refined socialising.

Horse
Born in 1954, 1966, 1978, 1990, 2002

Endowed with an amazing capacity for hard work and sustained endeavour. Determined, independent, intelligent and ambitious, with a strong will to succeed. Friendly and outgoing, with a good sense of humour and definite charisma. Always popular and well respected. However, can be somewhat selfish and egotistical on rare occasions.

Goat
Born in 1955, 1967, 1979, 1991, 2003

Elegant, suave and good natured, with a strong artistic streak. Favours strong family ties and is very loyal to close friends. Shies away from arguments and confrontations. Level-headed, considerate and patient. Enjoys material comforts and thrives on good company and good times. At times, has a tendency towards pessimism and complaint, but never for too long.

Monkey
Born in 1956, 1968, 1980, 1992, 2004

Witty, intelligent and versatile. Universally popular and well regarded, despite a penchant for mischief and trickery. Grasps every opportunity to excel and thrives on solving complex problems and meeting unforeseen challenges. Tends to move quickly from task to task, preferring a quick success to a lengthy endeavour. Usually successful and always entertaining.

Rooster
Born in 1957, 1969, 1981, 1993, 2005

Shrewd, hard working, positive and determined. Usually well organised, carefully prepared and well informed. Financially adroit and an astute investor. Extravagant and outgoing, enjoying praise and flattery, while resenting criticism. Sometimes boastful and flamboyant, yet never mean, dull or boring.

Dog
Born in 1958, 1970, 1982, 1994, 2006

Completely dependable, honest, trustworthy and noble. Unfailingly loyal to family and friends and a consistent supporter of truth and justice. Never forgives a slight or transgression. Predictable rather than flamboyant, consistent rather than versatile. At ease with all walks of life. Tends to worry too much.

Pig
Born in 1959, 1971, 1983, 1995, 2007

A shrewd mind and a sharp intellectual together with a firm grasp of practicalities. Welcomes challenges, difficult tasks and complicated problems. Honest, sincere and even-tempered with a keen nose for untruths. Very hospitable and sharing, but also rather materialistic and acquisitive. Can be rather naïve, somewhat disorganised and prone to gossip.

11
Basic Etiquette

On meeting

A short, light handshake and a brief nod is customary. A business card should be offered with both hands, the printing facing the recipient. Ideally, it should carry English on one side of the card, Chinese on the other (simplified characters for mainland China, full characters for elsewhere). Take more cards than you think you will possibly need! Study carefully any cards received before pocketing. Initial small talk can safely include family, food, job and money. Do not be surprised at frankness, especially concerning money. You may be asked how much your wristwatch/handbag/shoes cost. As in many other places, avoid discussion of politics and religion.

Knee ger sow bew, gen der wang gin ma?
Door see-how cheen?
Is your wristwatch real gold?
How much wast it?

Gifts

Personal gifts can include fruit, tea or flowers and are usually exchanged on meeting or at the beginning of a social function. Red or gold wrapping paper is auspicious. Avoid white or black. Present and receive gifts with both hands. Never give a clock as a gift. Avoid opening a gift in the presence of the giver. Do not be offended if the recipient of your gift initially declines to accept it.

Business meetings

Be punctual. More than ten minutes late is impolite. Rather than one-on-one, business meetings are usually formal gatherings round a table with refreshments, sometimes followed by a meal. Introductions will be in order of seniority, with a handshake followed by an exchange of business cards, small talk and tea, before getting down to business. Gifts are exchanged at the end of the meeting, with usually a main gift for the company as whole and smaller gifts for individuals.

Avoid expansive hand gestures, which are considered arrogant. Maintain eye contact with any interlocutor. A Chinese nod is not agreement, but an indication of attentive listening. Laughter can be a sign of nervousness or embarrassment. Rather than saying 'No', it could be suggested to you that something is difficult, under consideration or inconvenient (especially if followed by a sucking of breath through the teeth!). A hand waved close to the face indicates no, or a mild rebuke. To point with the forefinger is hostile. Modesty, patience and politeness are greatly valued. Business decisions are not usually spontaneous and may take some time. However, once taken, they are invariably honoured to the letter.

'Face' (*Mian Gee*)

Although the concept of 'face' is not unique to the Chinese, it is a key factor in any relationship. 'Face' is a person's perception of their dignity and status in the eyes of others. To receive praise, thanks or recommendation in front of other people, especially colleagues, gives face. Conversely, any public criticism, insult or embarrassment results in loss of face. Any such slight is difficult to forgive. Always remain polite, calm and complimentary. Any rebuke, reprimand or criticism should be given in private.

Dining

Arrive on time, suitably attired (check dress code with host), bearing appropriate gift and greet your host then others in order of seniority. The guest of honour will be seated opposite the host, usually at a round table seating eight or twelve. The host will start the meal by serving his main guest or announcing *'chee kwai zer'* (literally: pick up your chopsticks!) Pace yourself during the many courses, as to stop eating half way through the meal is an insult. The food is usually served on a large revolving Lazy Susan in the middle of the table. Guests rotate this at leisure, so time your lunge well to avoid missing your favourite dish until the next time round. Adjacent guests may place food on your plate as a politeness. To accept the food is sufficiently polite, you do not necessarily have to eat it.

When eating rice, lift the bowl to your mouth and use your chopsticks to scoop. Be prepared for and do not be offended by noisy eating and drinking habits. Toothpicks are liberally used (with the customary hand over the mouth) and also to assist with slippery morsels such as sea slugs and jelly fish slices. The meal ends when the host declares it over or you are given an orange.

Toasts will probably be drunk throughout the meal, usually in wine, brandy or mao tai. The latter is a fiery sourghum-derived spirit which should be respected. *Gan bay*! (Cheers!)

To use a knife and fork is not impolite, but you will gain 'face' by using chopsticks. Do not drop your chopsticks or lay them down crossing each other (bad luck). Do not point with them or use one to spear food (bad manners). It is safest to always lay them on the little chopstick rest usually provided to the right of your plate.

Joss

The Chinese, who love gambling, never underestimate the importance of 'joss'. Bad joss should be avoided and includes the colour white, dropped chopsticks, the number four and disturbing sleeping dragons and bad spirits. Good joss can be fostered by red and gold colours, the number eight and extensive 'wind and water' (*feng shoi*) precautions against dragons and the like.

12
Some Basic Vocabulary

A

accident	*shee goo*
acupuncture	*jen joo*
adaptor	*she pay chee*
after	*gee how*
afternoon	*siar woo*
again	*zai*
airport	*fey chee chang*
air conditioned	*yow kung tew*
all	*doe*
already	*ye jing*
all right, OK	*may gwan she*
also	*yer*
always	*chong sher*
ambassador	*dar sher*
ambulance	*joo hoo cher*
and	*her*
angry	*fen new*
answer	*dar foo*
antiques	*goo dung*
apples	*ping gwore*
April	*Ser Yewer*
at	*zai*
ATM machine	*chew kwan gee*

B

bad	*boo how*
baggage	*sing lee*
to bake	*cow shoe*
ballpoint pen	*yuan joo bee*

bank	*yin hang*
branch	*fen hang*
barber	*tee too jiang*
bathroom	*yew fang*
battery	*dian chee*
beautiful	*may lee*
because	*yin why*
bedroom	*woo sher*
beef	*new roo*
beer	*pea chew*
before	gee cheen
behind	*how mian*
beneath	*siar bian*
beside	*pang bian*
better	*geng how*
beware	*siaow seen*
bicycle	*gee sing cher*
big	*dar*
bill, account	*my dan*
bird	*niaow*
black	*hay ser*
blue	*lan ser*
body	*shen tea*
boiled rice	*buy fan*
book	*shoe*
bottled water	*ping jiang shui*
bread	*mian bow*
breakfast	*jow chan*
broken	*why ler*
brother	*ger ger*
brown	*jong ser*
brush	*shoe er*
bus	*gung gung chee cher*
bus stop	*cher jan*
businessman	*shang ren*

but	*dan sher*
butter	*whang yo*
to buy	*my*

C

cake	*dan gow*
camera	*jiao siang gee*
car	*chee cher*
carpet	*dee tan*
certainly, of course	*dang ren*
chair	*ye zer*
to change (money)	*wan*
cheap	*pea-hen ye*
cheers!	*gan bay!*
	(lit: dry glass)
cheese	*nai lao*
chemist shop	*wa swear jiang*
chicken	*gee roo*
Chinese (language)	*han yew*
chopsticks	*kwai zer*
cigarette	*siang yan*
cinema	*dian ying yuan*
city	*cheng she*
clean	*gan jing*
clever	*chong ming*
clock	*chong*
closed (store)	*gwan men*
clothing	*ye foo*
coast	*high bien*
coca cola	*core la*
coffee	*car fey*
cold	*leng*
college	*swear yuen*
colour	*yan ser*
comb	*shoe zer*

commerce	*shang yer*
complaint	*toe sue*
congratulations	*joo her*
consulate	*ling sher gwan*
country	*gwore jar*
crime	*joy sing*
crowd	*ren chun*
cup	*bay zer*
Customs & Excise	*high gwan*

D

dancing	*tiow woo*
dangerous	*way sian*
daughter	*new er*
day	*tian*
December	*Sher er Yewer*
delicious	*how cher*
dentist	*ya ye*
desert	*shar mo*
dictionary	*zer dian*
diesel	*chai yo*
difficult	*nan*
dining room	*fan ting*
dinner	*wan fan*
dirty	*jang der*
distance	*joo lee*
district	*chew*
doctor	*dai foo*
	(also *ye shang*)
dog	*go*
dollar	*may yuan*
double bed	*schwang ren chuang*
door	*men*
to drink	*her*
dry	*gan*

dry cleaning	*gan see*
duck	*ya zer*
dumplings	*jow zer*

E

each	*may ger*
early	*jow*
earth, land	*too*
east	*dong*
easy	*rong ye*
to eat	*cher*
egg	*gee dan*
electricity	*de-anne*
embassy	*dar sher gwan*
employee	*goo yuan*
empty	*kong*
engineer	*gong cheng sher*
English (language)	*ying yew*
entrance	*roo cow*
envelope	*sin feng*
especially	*you chee*
essential	*bee yew*
evening	*wan shang*
to enter	*gin roo*
every	*may ger*
exactly	*char char*
excellent	*hen how*
	(also: *fey chang gee how*)
exit	*chew cow*
expensive	*gow jar der*
	(also: *gwooi*)
excuse me (interrupting)	*lao jar*
excuse me (to get past)	*ching wen*
eye	*yan jing*

F

family	*jar ting*
far, distant	*yuan*
fare	*piaow jar*
fast (speed)	*kwai*
fat, obese	*pang*
father	*foo cheen*
fax	*chuan gen*
few	*han shao*
film (for camera)	*jow pea-hen*
film (movie)	*de-anne ying*
final, last	*joy how*
finger	*shao zer*
fish	*you*
to fly	*fay sing*
fly, midge	*chang ying*
flowers	*waar*
food	*sher woo*
forbidden	*gin gee*
foreign	*why gwore*
to forget	*wang gee*
fork	*char zer*
free, gratis	*mian fey*
fried rice	*chow fan*
friend	*peng yo*
fruit	*shoi gwore*
fruit juice	*gwore zer*
fuel	*ren lieu*
full	*man*

G

gate	*men*
generous	*dar fang*
gift	*lee woo*

girl	*new high*
glad, happy	*gow sing*
glass (drinking)	*bow lee bay*
to go	*chew*
gold	*wang gin*
golf	*gow er foo*
good	*how*
good bye	*zai gen*
good evening (on leaving)	*wan shang how*
good morning	*jow*
government	*jeng foo*
green	*loo ser*
green tea	*loo char*
guard	*jing way*
guest	*ker ren*
guidebook	*loo yo shoe*

H
hair	*too far*
hairbrush	*shoe zer*
hairdresser	*lee far sher*
half	*ye ban*
hand	*shoe*
hamburger	*han bow bow*
happy	*kwai ler*
harbour	*high gang*
hat	*mao zer*
to have	*yow*
headache	*too tong*
health, healthy	*jian kang*
heart	*seen*
heavy	*chung*
hello	*knee how*
help, aid	*bang chew*

her, him	*ta*
here	*jer lee*
high	*gow*
to hire	*goo young*
history	*lee sher*
holiday	*jar chee*
honest	*cheng she*
horse	*ma*
hot	*rer*
hot (spicey)	*laa*
hotel	*loo gwan*
	(also: *fan diane*)
hour	*siaow sher*
house	*fang zer*
how are you?	*knee how?*
how much?	*door siaow cheen?*
hungry	*er ler*
hurry up!	*gan gin*
husband	*jang foo*
hygienic	*way sheng*

I

I, me	*war*
ice	*bing*
ID card	shen *fen jeng*
if	*roo gwore*
ill	*yo bing*
immediately	*ma shang*
important	*jong yew*
information	*sin see*
inside	*nay boo*
international	*gwore gee*
invitation	*yow ching*
island	*dao*

J

jasmine tea	*more lee wah char*
January	*Ye yewer*
jewellery	*joo bow*
job	*gong jaw*
journalist	*sin when*

K

key	*yow sher*
kilometre	*gong lee*
kindness	*how ye*
knife	*dow*
knife and fork	*dow char*
to know something	*chee dao*
to know, to be able	*wooi*
to know a person	*ren sher*

L

last, final	*joy how*
late	*wan*
law	*far ling*
lazy	*lan*
leader	*leng sue*
left	*jaw*
leg	*toy*
lemon	*ning meng*
library	*too shoe gwan*
light (electric)	*deng*
light (weight)	*ching*
to like	*sea wan*
a little	*ye dee ar*
to look around	*can ye can*
luggage	*sing lee*
lunch	*woo chan*

M

machine	*gee chee*
mad	*feng*
magazine	*jar gee*
man	*nan ren*
manager	*jing lee*
many	*han door*
map	*dee too*
March	*San Yewer*
market	*sher chang*
married	*jer hun der*
may	*woo yewer*
maybe	*ker neng*
me	*war*
meal	*chan*
meaning	*ye ser*
to meet	*jian mian*
meeting	*huey ye*
melon	*gwar*
menu	*cha dan*
message	*seen sea*
meter	*bee-how*
metre	*me*
middle	*jung yang*
milk	*new nigh*
million	*buy wan*
minute (time)	*fen jong*
mistake	*chore woo*
modern	*sea-hen dye*
money	*cheen*
month	*yewer*
moon	*yewer liang*
morning	*shang woo*
mosquito	*wen zer*

mother	*moo cheen*
mountain	*shan*
Mr	*seen shang*
Mrs	*tie tie*
Miss	*new sher*

N

name	*ming zer*
to need, to want	*yew*
neighbour	*lin joo*
new	*seen der*
news, information	*seen when*
newspapers	*bow gee*
night	*yer*
noisy	*swan waa*
non-smoking	*boo see yan*
noon	*jong woo*
north	*bay boo*
notebook	*bee gee ban*
november	*sher ye yewer*
now	*sea-hen zai*
number (room, 'phone)	*shoe zer*
	(also: *how*)

O

of course, certainly	*dang ran*
office (building)	*ban gong sher*
oh dear!	*aye yar!*
	(also: *waar!*)
oil	*yo*
old	*lao*
onions	*yang chong*
only	*gee*
open	*kai*

opportunity	*gee wooi*
or	*wore*
oranges	*cheng*
other	*chee tar der*
outside	*way boo*

P

pain	*teng tong*
paper	*gee*
passenger	*cheng ker*
passport	*who jao*
peaceful, quiet	*ping jing*
pen	*bee*
people	*ren*
pepper	*who jow fen*
perfume	*shang shoi*
to permit, allow	*ker ye*
petrol	*sher yo*
photograph	*siang pea-hen*
pills	*yow*
place	*dee fang*
please	*cheng.....*
police	*jing fang*
policeman	*jing char*
police station	*jing char chew*
pork	*chew roo*
porter	*ban yun gong*
possible	*ker neng*
to post mail	*yo gee*
post office	*you chew*
potatoes	*too do*
present, current	*moo cheen*
present, gift	*lee woo*
to press, iron	*yun tang*

principal, main	*joo yow der*
problem	*when tee*
prohibited	*gin gee ger*
price	*jar ger*

Q
question	*when tee*
quickly	*kwai*

R
railway station	*wore cher jan*
rain	*you*
razor blades	*tee sue dow dow*
	pea-hen
ready, prepared	*jun bay*
receptionist	*jer dye yuan*
recently	*joy gin*
red	*hung ser*
to rent, hire	*chew zoo*
repair	*sew lee how*
reply	*wooi dar*
to reserve, a reservation	*you deng*
rest, nap	*sieu see sieu see*
restaurant	*chan gwan*
(also: *fan gwan,* colloquial: *gwan zer*)	
result	*jer gwore*
to return	*fan wooi*
rice	*me fan*
rich	*yow cheen*
right (not left)	*you*
right, correct	*jeng chew*
river	*her*
rmb (people's currency)	*yuan*
	(colloquial: *kwai*)

room (hotel)	*fang jian*
room charge	*fang fey*
roasted	*cow*

S

sad	*bay shang*
safe (adjective)	*anne chuan*
safe (noun)	*bow sian goy*
salad	*sir la*
salt	*yan*
sand	*shar*
sandwich	*san meng gee*
to say, speak	*shore*
sea	*high*
seat, chair	*ye zer*
secretary	*me shoe*
to see	*can*
to send	*song*
shampoo	*see far jing*
shirt	*chen shan*
shoes	*sea air*
shops	*shang de-anne*
short	*aye*
shut	*gwan*
side	*bien*
silver	*yin*
sister (older)	*jer jer*
sister (younger)	*may may*
sit down	*chore*
slow	*man*
slow down!	*man dee, man dee!*
small	*siaow*
smoking prohibited	*boo jin see yin*
sometimes	*yow sher*

son	*er zer*
soon	*kwai*
sorry	*doi boo chee*
soup	*tang*
to speak	*schwore*
spectacles	yan jing
spoon	*showe zer*
sport	*yuan dung*
stairs	*loo tee*
stamp (postage)	*yo piaow*
star	*sing*
station	*jan*
stomach ache	*do zer teng*
stop the car!	*teng cher!*
swimming pool	*you yong chee*
switch on	*kai*
switch off	*gwan dieu*

T

table	*chore zer*
table tennis	*ping pang chew*
taxi	*dick sea*
tea	*char*
tea cup	*char bey*
technical	*gee shoe sing*
technique	*fang far*
telephone	*diane wah*
to telephone	*da diane wah*
television	*diane sher*
temperature	*wen dar*
tennis	*wang chew*
temple	*miaow you*
terracotta soldiers	*bing ma yong*
thank you	*share share knee*

thank you (for gift or service)	*door jer knee*
there is	*yow*
there is not	*may yow*
they, them	*ta men*
that	*nar ger*
theatre	*joo chang*
there	*nar lee*
thing	*dong sea*
thirsty	*ker*
this	*jer ger*
thousand	*che-anne*
ticket	*piaow*
time (period)	*she jan*
time (occasion)	*chee*
tired	*hen lay*
to	*dow*
today	*gin tian*
toilet	*chee sore*
toilet paper	*way sheng gee*
tomato (northern China)	*see hong sher*
tomato (southern China)	*fan ker*
tomorrow	*ming tian*
tooth ache	*yar teng*
toothbrush	*yar shoe er*
toothpaste	*yar gow*
tourist	*loo yo jer*
tourist information office	*loo yo gee lieu chew*
towel	*mao gin*
town	*gen*
train (railway)	*wore cher*
to travel	*loo sing*
travel agency	*loo sing sher*
traveller's cheques	*loo sing gee pew*
trousers	*koo zer*

true	*jen der*
to understand	*ming buy*

U

useful	*yo young*
us, we	*war men*
usual, usually	*tong chang*

V

vacant, empty	*kong*
vegetables	*shoe chai*
very	*hen*
video camera	*loo siang gee*
VIP	*yow ren*
to visit	*yow lan*
visa	*cheen jeng*
visitor	*ker ren*

W

to wait	*deng*
to walk	*boo sing*
wallet	*cheen bow*
water	*shoi*
to wear	*chuan*
weary	*kun far*
week	*sing chee*
weather	*tian chee*
weight	*jong liang*
welcome	*wan ying*
west	*sea*
what?	*shen mer?*
when?	*shen mer she how?*
where?	*nar?*
which?	*nar ger?*
who?	*shay?*

white	*buy ser*
why?	*way shen mer?*
wife	*chee zer*
wind	*feng*
window	*chuang who*
wine	*poo tow chew*
winter	*dung tian*
with	*tung*
without	*may yo*
woman	*new ren*
work	*gong jaw*
world	*she jer*
writing paper	*sin gee*
wrong, error	*chore*

Y

year	*nian*
yellow	*wang ser*
yes	*doi*
yesterday	*jaw tian*
you	*knee*
you (plural)	*knee men*
young	*nian ching*

Z

| zero | *ling* |
| zoo | *dong wu yuan* |

Other titles in the *'Very Simple...'* series

Very Simple Arabia by James Peters

Very Simple Arabic by James Peters

Very Simple Arabic Script by James Peters